Poems From My Soul

Diane Alexy

Copyright © 2017 Diane Alexy

All rights reserved.

ISBN: 1544172508
ISBN-13: 978-1544172507

DEDICATION

This book is dedicated to my beloved grandmother, who created a world in which I felt truly loved and who inspired me to start writing poems from my soul at age 10. Thank you nana for your bright light of love, which shaped and sustained my spirit.

TABLE OF CONTENTS

NATURE
Night and Day	Page 3
The Beach	Page 4
The Churchyard	Page 5
Convergence	Page 6
The Gulf of Mexico	Page 7
Ode to Flowers	Page 8
Night	Page 9

LOVE
Loved	Page 13
Eyes of Love	Page 14
I Can't Say	Page 15
Unbroken	Page 16
Love Is	Page 17
You Live On	Page 18

POETRY
A Poem	Page 21
My Poetry	Page 22
My Path	Page 23

FAMILY
To Nana	Page 27
Cousin Pamela	Page 28
To Eric	Page 29
The Baby	Page 30

TABLE OF CONTENTS (continued)

SEASONS
Seasons	Page 33
Spring	Page 34
Summer Love	Page 35
Fall	Page 36
Winter Trees	Page 37

HUMOR
Tomorrow	Page 41
Perspective	Page 42
Worrying Less	Page 43

SPIRITUAL
Reflections	Page 47
Prayer	Page 48
Ascent	Page 49
The Only Day	Page 50
Why	Page 51

SUNDRY
Colors	Pages 55-56
NYC 9/11	Page 57
Prejudice	Page 58

ABOUT THE AUTHOR　　Page 59

ACKNOWLEDGEMENTS

I would like to express my appreciation to my cousin Pamela for being such a big fan of my poetry and a treasured member of my family.

I am also very thankful to have such a wonderful friend, John, a talented musician and a poet himself. His praise of my verse, his sense of humor, and his encouragement have made a big difference in my life.

Thanks to my friend Claudia for always being there to listen to my latest creations and give me a thumbs up.

Thanks also to Dawn, who swears that she is the biggest fan of my poetry—and she just may be right! Thank you for applauding my poems and insisting that I really must share them with the world.

I'm very grateful to Tom for sharing his delightful poetry and for listening with his heart to my creations. He inspired me to write many of my best verses.

I want to thank Garrett for motivating me to write my own book of poetry after reading his wonderful books. I'm so grateful that he lent a helping hand by sharing his knowledge of publishing. I wish him well with his poetry, playwriting and acting.

Thank you too, Mary D., for always being so positive about my poetry and giving me the gift of a lovely journal to write more poems in. I miss you and I hope your life changes have brought you happiness.

Poetry Time

Please do indulge my poet's soul
    And care to share my calling
        My heartfelt rhythmic words I hope
            On open hearts are falling

                        Diane Alexy

NATURE

Night and Day

The stars are scattered far away
They came out with the moon to play

The sun is somewhere shining bright
But here now it's the realm of night

The dawn will then erase the dark
And sun will blaze from just a spark

The stars and sun make their return
When night and day each take their turn

The Beach

The scent of sea arouses now
  joyful anticipation
    of crashing waves upon the shore
     and shells and rock formations

Of wet, soft sand between one's toes
  of sea birds calling sweetly
    of distant vistas where the sky
     and sea meet non-discretely

And if, by chance, it is day's end
  the sunset will then treat us
    to a vision of the heaven that
     one day I hope will greet us

The Churchyard

I pass the churchyard when I must
Which of late is every day
Since spring is now residing there
My heart leads me back this way

The daffodils are golden gems
And the hyacinths are sublime
The croci sadly disappeared
To return in their good time

The cherry tree is thriving now
With frilly blossoms looming
Serrated tulips, full of life,
Are in vibrant colors blooming

Convergence

I felt the rain cry with me
  Tears falling from the sky

The wind seemed to be sad too
  Along with me it sighed

Dark storm clouds rose within me
  As bleak as those on high

My soul converged with nature
  That day I said goodbye

The Gulf of Mexico

Bright sun stars twinkle on this sea
Which strokes the shore eternally
Cloudless blue of sky embracing
Frostless snow of sand displacing

When then the blaze of sunset burns
This undulating mass quite turns
The pigment of a bright peach hue
Suspending briefly what is true

As nightfall dims my balcony
I stand in timeless reverie
The moonlit surf resounding far
Communing with a sparkling star

Transcending my mortality
I merge with vast infinity
Attaining cosmic peace inside
I flow serenely with the tide

Ode to Flowers

Flowers suffuse our senses
With their lovely hues and scent
So fresh and beautiful they seem
From heaven to be sent

They add joy when we celebrate
The special times in life
As on the very happy day
A bride becomes a wife

On some occasions we give them
As gifts to show our love
And they commiserate when souls
Are called to home above

Labors of love from mother earth
They're treasures on display
Creating seventh heaven with
A beautiful bouquet

 Night

The splendor of the setting sun
Adds glory to day's end
Daylight melts into darkness now
And night falls once again

The moon and stars step on the stage
In their nocturnal role
Denying nighttime total dark
Their tranquil light they dole

On summer nights a calm befalls
When crickets serenade
And glowing lights of fireflies
Surprise then quickly fade

In winter, nights are fast to fall
And cold and winds distress
When safely in the warmth of home
We are among the blessed

LOVE

Loved

Like the glowing golden sun
Warmth filled me to the core
Like a bird in God's blue sky
On wings my soul now soared

Like gardens filled with spring
I felt renewed and pretty
Like kittens drunk with youth
I felt carefree and giddy

Like the tallest mountain peak
My heart was lifted high
Like a rushing waterfall
I flowed with joy inside

And I found heaven then
As in the sky above me
When hearing those sweet words
That day you said you loved me

Eyes of Love

Your eyes are warm and shining bright
  Like jewels of topaz blue
    Their passion has me mesmerized
    They show your love is true

I know that when you look at me
  You see in my eyes too
    The deep love that is also there
    And in my heart for you

I Can't Say

I can't say how much I love you
It's not that I haven't tried
I'm not keeping it a secret
Love is not something to hide

If I simply say I love you
Then I would have somewhat lied
Even my poet's way with words
Can't express such love inside

Unbroken

Unbroken cords of love remain
They cannot ever fade
When love is true the bond's as strong
As on the day it's made

Death cannot end eternal love
It lives within our souls
Connecting us through different worlds
We need but to behold

Love Is

Love is a waterfall uniting with the
blue beneath in exhilaration

Love is sweet tenderness captured in the
magic of the moment

Love is a burst of lightning
preceded by the fall of gentle rain

Love is the anchor that keeps a soul
from drifting away from godliness

You Live On

I love you in the morning
  And in the afternoon
    I love you in cold winter
      And in the heat of June

I think about you often
  And though you're gone today
    Because my heart remembers
      You'll never pass away

POETRY

A Poem

A poem's a poet's child

Conceived and carried with care

Brought to term and born then

To hold and love and share

My Poetry

I search my soul and write what's there

The timeless truth I shape and share

And hopefully my soul finds yours

And touches it so that it soars

My Path

Poetry is my innate goal
  It stirs with passion in my soul

I record the truth and joys I know
  Which in the lives of others flow

And seek my verse to thus create
  A truth to which good souls relate

FAMILY

To Nana

My sweet gentle nana, your love in my life
Gave me the strength to prevail amidst strife
Your goodness and kindness shone through in your care
At peace in your arms I felt safe, without fear

My world was so blessed to be filled with your light
You taught me that love is what makes a life right
I'm thankful to you for the treats and the praise
For creating such joyful and beautiful days

Your glorious garden with pansies so bright
And fragrant rose arbor filled me with delight
The muguet des bois perfume that you favored
Summons sweet memories of you that I savor

Your light in my deep core shines brightly today
Recalling your humor, I smile at your play
You live on within me; we will never part
Your pure love enduring in my grateful heart

Your memory is cherished and will so remain
The depth of my true love for you will not wane
Your beautiful spirit has made you so dear
I pray, when my time comes, that you will be there

Cousin Pamela

A charming child held so dear
Her precious portrait without peer
Angelic in her frills of white
Bright eyes aglow with God's pure light

From first we met my heart she won
Her loveliness like rays of sun
A gift, I thought, from up above
Her grace like magic kindled love

The childhood bond so sweet is clear
Of true love that is still quite there
The cherished girl of yesterday
A winsome woman loved today

Author holding Pamela

To Eric

A nephew nearly son to me
You're loving and so kind
I'm blessed you are part of my life
Through family ties that bind

Your calling to rush in to help
Exposes you to danger
Your strong and very caring soul
To bravery not a stranger

I'm very proud of your success
In work and choice of wife
As a father you provide
For happiness in life

Thank you for the many times
You've sweetly said "I love you"
In verse I want to say how much
My heart is filled with love too

The Baby

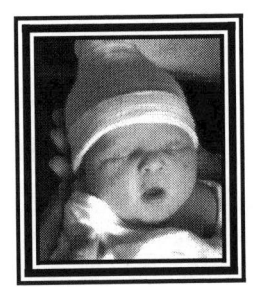

With care and love my family waits
Is it a boy or girl?
Who we will take into our hearts
And welcome to this world

The long-awaited birth day comes
And then the joyful guests
A beautiful, sweet baby girl
In mother's arms now rests

I view with awe this gift from God
With tiny hands and toes
Who sleeps in perfect peacefulness
An innocent only knows

And when, as nana, in my arms
An angel I enfold
My heart flows with a pure love for
This precious life I hold

SEASONS

Seasons

The great green true I love so well
is now a golden hue
   The artist nature painted it
   an autumn color true

I do prefer her palette green
but now a change is due
   And soon the gold will too be gone
   as winter takes its cue

Then from the buds of welcomed spring
great works of art ensue
   When mother nature paints again
   the blossoms born anew

Spring

The season that I hold most dear
When earth's renewal is so fair
When barren winter takes its leave
And birds chant songs from budding trees

Precocious crocuses unfold
In amethyst and citrine gold
Of tender growth there is no dearth
Fresh blossoms fill the fertile earth

A cherry tree's a joy to view
With frilly blooms of soft pink hue
Sustaining showers come and go
Assuring nature's gifts will grow

The sky appears then pure in hue
Of infinite, celestial blue
My spirit soars in days of spring
When earth's rebirth such beauty brings

Summer Love

The summer sadly fades
   as cool days of lessened light

Turn into fall with leaves
   in bright colors taking flight

When next the frigid winds
   swirl in storms of winter white

I yearn then for return
   of loved summer warm and bright

Fall

Fall holds us in its cool embrace
And quells the summer's laid-back pace
Gone are the warmer, lengthy days
But fall, too, has its worthy ways

Stout pumpkins turned to tasty fare
Invigorating autumn air
Great feasts whereby thanks we attest
To all the ways we have been blessed

Fall's blazing leaves are works of art
Of once-green trees that rift apart
As nature seeks itself to bare
And for more bitter times prepare

Winter Trees

Trees bare and cold, stark in the lessened light of winter. Trees devoid of the joy of spring, the green of summer, and the glory of the palette of fall. Snowflakes then fall from the heavens, and the trees, adorned now in pure and sparkling white, reclaim themselves as objects of beauty.

HUMOR

Tomorrow

I said I would do it tomorrow
And I meant it with all of my heart
But then I woke up the next morning
And realized a new day did start

So it now was today not tomorrow
So my promise to do what I hate
I needn't have to worry to do yet
Cause I said for tomorrow I'd wait

Perspective

I've come to now realize
That perspective is key
To if we enjoy life
Or its misery see

As the wise saying goes
When life's lemons have played
We can fret sour moments
Or enjoy lemonade

The more years I live now
The more I want less
To heed tribulations
And cause myself stress

I'll no longer let woes
My composure attack
So sipping that fruit ade
I'll enjoy life laid-back

Worrying Less

I find as I get older

Less worried I now get

But then I think that maybe

To worry I now forget!

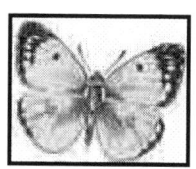

SPIRITUAL

Reflections

I reflect now on life
And what I have done
And the things I have lost
And those I have won

And my raison d'etre
Here on this good earth
My mission to realize
The goal of my birth

Beyond sharing my heart
In love and in care
I feel destined to leave
The earthly mark here

Of a part of myself
The essence of me
That I will bequeath
In my soul's poetry

Prayer

Bathe us in the light of love
Which renders dark and hatred weak
Bless us with the gift of hope
So we will not despair but seek

Fill our hearts with courage fierce
So we can live our dreams of life
Bless us with the gift of peace
That will then still our inner strife

Fill our souls with faith supreme
So we perceive what we can't see
And let our lives be filled with joy
As days on earth were meant to be

Ascent

We climb with joy and peril
  Life's rocky mountain face

We feel exhilarated
  When we can move apace

But sometimes rocks will loosen
  Ascent no longer safe

And we must change direction
  And find another space

To gain a better foothold
  To serve now as our base

Then when secure to forge ahead
  Grateful for the grace

Harm averted, there's the chance
  To reach a higher place

The Only Day

Today is the only day that will ever exist on this day of this month of this year. Once it is over we will never have the chance to live it again.
It is unique in its place in the string of days that comprise our time on this earth. To see it as the once in a lifetime opportunity that it is makes it special. We should try to fill it with as much joy and love, accomplishment and giving as we can. Each special day, lived to the fullest, combined with all other special days, makes for a life well-lived.

Why

With passion I will pass this way

My time on earth intense

With hope and care I'll spend some time

Just trying to make sense

Of why this world contains such vice

When love should fill each heart

And why God's gift of our free will

Has torn our peace apart

SUNDRY

 Colors

Green is the color of boundless leaves
Which decorate the splendid trees
From my window I love to view
Lush in their sunlit verdant hue

Blue is the color children ask why
When curious about the hue of sky
The deep blue is used to describe
The vast sea in eternal tide

Red, the rich color of our blood,
Courses through us in a flood
So vital to us that we give
Donations to help others live

Yellow is seen in glowing sun
A warmer, brighter hue there's none
Our spirits are lifted with its light
When golden dawn brings end to night

Purple, I think, is at its best
In jewels of sparkling amethyst
To further grant it what it's due
I'll laud the lilac's lovely hue

 (continued)

Another gemstone comes to mind
Of a very pretty green blue kind
The Caribbean Sea is of this hue
A vast and tranquil turquoise view

Lily-white means clean as snow
Opposed to what is base and low
White represents goodness and light
Angels waft on wings of white

A dark and somber hue is black
Linked with evil, but here's a fact
How else would stars appear so bright
Were it not for the black of night?

I once read orange is perverse
I'll not agree here in this verse
How can such insult it be paid?
No bad decisions it has made

And now my favorite one of all
With which of late I've been enthralled
A bright and happy hue I think
Is springtime, cherry blossom pink

NYC 9/11

A nightmare scores the morning sky
Crushed with grief, we ask but why
The mighty twins come tumbling down
In ash and rubble to the ground

We hear the cries; we feel the fear
Too many lost we hold so dear
We cannot grasp what we are told
Of men gone mad, who have no soul

With broken hearts we carry on
Our peace of mind for now is gone
Lord, help us to defeat this hate
Before, again, it is too late

Prejudice

We should walk this earth together
Whether yellow, black or white
Is it sensible to judge someone
Based merely on our sight?

It's the soul that is important
How much one loves and cares
And whether with propriety
One handles life's affairs

ABOUT THE AUTHOR

In September of 2012, Diane was very honored to be awarded a rare old book of poetry by the director of Nomad's Choir on the day she read as a new poet to the group. Diane has since had several of her poems, including **The Baby**, published in the *Nomad's Choir Poetry Journal*.

In May of 2013, Diane was Poet of the Month at The New York Poetry Forum.

Diane has also been privileged to read her poetry to members of the Women's Welsh New York City Club and to have had her poems, including **Unbroken**, published in the group's monthly newsletters. One of her nature photographs was posted on the Club's website.

Most recently her poem, **Perspective**, was published in the 2017 *7 Train Anthology*.

Made in the USA
Columbia, SC
01 August 2017